12 UNSOLVED
MYSTERIES

by Brandon Terrell

STORY
LIBRARY

www.12StoryLibrary.com

12-Story Library is an imprint of Peterson Publishing Company and Press Room Editions.

Produced for 12-Story Library by Red Line Editorial

Photographs ©: Harris & Ewing/Library of Congress, cover, 1; Henry Howe, 4; North Wind Picture Archives, 5; Ursatii/Shutterstock Images, 7, 29; Walter Edwin Frost, 8; Major James Skitt Matthews, 9; appletat/iStockphoto, 10; Anneka/Shutterstock Images, 11; Lightguard/iStockphoto, 12; Lt. Comdr. Horace Bristol/US Navy, 13; Underwood and Underwood/Library of Congress, 14; Acme Newspictures/New York World-Telegram and the Sun Newspaper Photograph Collection/Library of Congress, 15; Kunal Mehta/Shutterstock Images, 17, 28; HO/AP Images, 18; AP Images, 19, 22; Samantha Marx CC2.0, 20; Albo/Shutterstock Images, 21; Nickolay Vinokurov/Shutterstock Images, 24; Svetlana Arapova/Shutterstock Images, 25; Franklin D. Roosevelt/US National Archives and Records Administration, 27

Library of Congress Cataloging-in-Publication Data
Names: Terrell, Brandon, 1978- author.
Title: 12 unsolved mysteries / by Brandon Terrell.
Other titles: Twelve unsolved mysteries
Description: Mankato, MN : 12-Story Library, 2017. | Series: Scary and spooky
  | Includes bibliographical references and index.
Identifiers: LCCN 2016002358 (print) | LCCN 2016006724 (ebook) | ISBN
  9781632352989 (library bound : alk. paper) | ISBN 9781632353481 (pbk. :
  alk. paper) | ISBN 9781621434641 (hosted ebook)
Subjects: LCSH: Parapsychology--Juvenile literature. | Curiosities and
  wonders--Juvenile literature. | History--Miscellanea--Juvenile literature.
Classification: LCC BF1031 .T38 2016 (print) | LCC BF1031 (ebook) | DDC
  001.94--dc23
LC record available at http://lccn.loc.gov/2016002358

Printed in the United States of America
Mankato, MN
May, 2016

Access free, up-to-date content on this topic plus a full digital version of this book. Scan the QR code on page 31 or use your school's login at 12StoryLibrary.com.

Table of Contents

Whole Colony of Settlers Disappears 4

Glowing UFOs Surround WWII Aircraft 6

Ghost Ship Adrift in the Arctic 8

Two Sisters Return From the Dead 10

Lost in the Bermuda Triangle 12

Famed Aviator Amelia Earhart Vanishes 14

Blobs of Goop Drop From the Sky 16

Man Leaps From Plane and Disappears 18

Three Men Escape From Alcatraz 20

Ship Found Sailing Without Crew Members 22

The Curse of the Evil Crater 24

Lost Treasure Hidden on Oak Island 26

Fact Sheet 28

Glossary 30

For More Information 31

Index 32

About the Author 32

Whole Colony of Settlers Disappears

In the spring of 1587, a ship containing a group of English men, women, and children set sail across the Atlantic Ocean. The ship was under the command of James White. It was bound for Chesapeake Bay. With hurricane season approaching, the ship instead made land on a small island off the coast of what is now North Carolina. The island was named Roanoke.

The colony was the first English settlement in the New World. White became the settlement's governor.

His granddaughter, Virginia Dare, was the first English child born in America. But times grew hard for the settlement. White sailed back to England for supplies and food.

A naval war between England and Spain delayed White's return to the colony. Three years passed before he could return. When he arrived at Roanoke in August 1590, he found the settlement abandoned. There was no trace of the colonists. Only one possible clue to their fate was discovered. A word, carved into a

The Roanoke colonists gather together for Virginia Dare's baptism.

116

Approximate number of English settlers to arrive at Roanoke Island.

- James White was the settlement's governor.
- White traveled back to England for additional supplies and spent three years there before returning to America.
- One mysterious clue to the missing colonists remained: the word *CROATOAN*.
- Remains have been found suggesting the colonists may have joined an American Indian tribe.

The only clue left behind from the settlers was a single word.

wooden post: *CROATOAN*. But what did it mean? And where were the settlers?

Numerous theories about the fate of the Roanoke settlers have been suggested over the years. Croatoan was the name of an island south of Roanoke. It was also the name of the American Indian tribe who lived there. Some believe that this tribe attacked the settlement. Another theory suggests that the struggling colonists abandoned their camp in their own attempt to sail back to England.

Recently, archeological teams may have found remains that suggest the colonists survived and joined American Indian tribes. Metal bars and blocks believed to be European were found at a Croatoan forest site. Pottery and tools were found at a site 50 miles (80 km) from the settlement.

These findings offer clues to the mystery of the vanished Roanoke colony. However, the truth may never be known, making the lost settlers of Roanoke one of America's oldest unsolved mysteries.

Glowing UFOs Surround WWII Aircraft

During World War II (1939–1945), the skies were a battleground. Enemy planes often flew through the dark skies firing shots. But soldiers also reported seeing a series of unidentified flying objects (UFOs) in the air throughout the war.

Reports started in September 1941 from British pilots. Glowing objects were following or flying next to aircraft. One soldier described them as disc-like. The objects became known as Foo Fighters. The spheres appeared as small, metallic globes during the day. But at night they glowed in various colors.

British, German, Japanese, and US pilots and aircrews all claimed to have seen Foo Fighters. The objects never made contact with any planes. And despite being fired upon, none of the Foo Fighters were ever damaged.

Despite these sightings, there are very few quality photos of the mysterious objects. Many theories attempt to explain the lights. Some say the lights were electrical discharges from an airplane's wings, or possibly ball lightning. But the truth behind the lights is still unknown.

51
Number of the US Air Force facility where UFOs are allegedly stored and studied.

- Glowing objects were first reported flying near WWII aircraft in 1941.
- The objects became known as Foo Fighters.
- The glowing orbs never made contact with any planes.
- There are few quality photos of the glowing lights and no explanation for them.

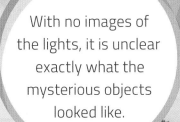

With no images of the lights, it is unclear exactly what the mysterious objects looked like.

THINK ABOUT IT

Thirty-six percent of Americans believe in UFOs. Do you? Conduct research online to support your opinion.

Ghost Ship Adrift in the Arctic

Captain John Cornwell and his crew set sail on the *Baychimo* on July 6, 1931. The cargo ship departed from Vancouver, Canada. It was destined for northern Alaska. The *Baychimo* had made this trip nine times before. But this July 1931 trip would be its last.

The *Baychimo* had neared its destination in early October. But the Arctic Ocean was choked with ice. The ship did not have enough room to navigate. Cornwell and his crew had to leave the ship. Rescue planes brought the men supplies. Some men were flown to the nearest town. The rest stayed behind and set up camp nearby. They hoped to rescue the *Baychimo* once some of the ice had shifted.

A blizzard hit the men's campsite in late November. The men searched for their ship after the storm had cleared. But it was nowhere to be

The *Baychimo* sits at the dock in Vancouver before its next trip.

The *Baychimo* was unable to move through the thick ocean ice.

found. Cornwell and his crew were never able to find the ship. But there were many reported sightings of the *Baychimo* years after its disappearance. The last reported sighting was in 1969. Some reported that they boarded the ship. But none were able to sail the ship out of the Arctic.

The Alaskan government started a formal search for the ship in 2006.

But they never found it. They called off the search in 2012. Exactly where the *Baychimo* is now remains a mystery.

1,322
Weight, in tons (1,200 metric tons), of the *Baychimo*.

- Captain John Cornwell and his crew set sail on the *Baychimo* in July 1931.
- Ice drifts in the Arctic Ocean stalled the ship in early October 1931.
- Cornwell and his crew searched for the ship after a blizzard in late November but were unable to find it.
- The Alaskan government started a search for the ship in 2006 but never found it.

THE USS *JEANNETTE*

Many ships besides the *Baychimo* have gone missing in the Arctic Ocean. One of the first was the USS *Jeannette*. The *Jeannette* set sail from San Francisco, California, in 1879. Its goal was to reach the North Pole. Its crew did not succeed. They were forced to abandon the ship. The ship sank off the north coast of Russia. It has not yet been found.

Two Sisters Return From the Dead

In May 1957, in the small town of Hexham, England, two young sisters were tragically killed. Six-year-old Jacqueline Pollock and her 11-year-old sister Joanna were out walking with a friend when a car struck them. All three died.

The sisters' parents, John and Florence Pollock, were devastated. More than a year passed and Florence gave birth to healthy twin girls named Gillian and Jennifer. John immediately believed the twins were the souls of their lost sisters.

Several unsolved mysteries and urban legends involve twins.

John noticed that Jennifer had a faint white scar across her forehead. It was in the same place Jacqueline had one caused by a bicycle accident. Jennifer also had a birthmark on her leg identical to one on Jacqueline's leg.

The unexplained similarities went further than that, however. Shortly after Jennifer and Gillian's birth, the Pollocks moved away from Hexham. They returned when the girls were four years old. The twins could correctly identify landmarks they had never seen before. Florence even found the twins playing a bizarre game. One sister pretended to be hit and injured by a car.

Gillian and Jennifer's odd behavior and memories vanished at the age of five. They went on to have a normal childhood. The Pollocks have insisted they did not tell the twins about their sisters' deaths until after the strange behavior. So was it all a coincidence? Or had the souls of the dead Pollock sisters returned in the form of their twin sisters? The truth will never be known.

The twins correctly named old toys and teddy bears that had belonged to their sisters.

24
Percent of Americans who believe in reincarnation.

- Twin sisters Gillian and Jennifer Pollock were born more than a year after the accidental death of their sisters.
- Their father believed the twins were the reincarnated souls of their dead sisters.
- One of the twins had a similar scar and birthmark as her deceased sister.
- Without being told, the twins seemed to remember places and things they had never known before.

Lost in the Bermuda Triangle

The vast oceans on Earth hold many mysteries. Among them is a stretch of the Atlantic Ocean. It reaches from the island of Bermuda to Puerto Rico to the southeastern tip of Florida. This expanse of water is known as the Bermuda Triangle.

This area has been the site of 20 plane and more than 50 ship disappearances. One famous incident happened in March 1918. The USS *Cyclops*, a navy cargo ship, disappeared in the Bermuda Triangle. The ship was 542 feet (165 m) long. It was carrying more than 300 men. A call for help from the *Cyclops* was never issued. There was a massive search, but the ship's wreckage was never found.

Years later, on December 5, 1945, five US Navy bomber planes took off from Fort Lauderdale, Florida. They carried 14 men. Soon the planes' compasses began to break down. The mission leader became lost. All five planes flew until their fuel ran out. They were forced to land in the water. A rescue plane and its 13-man crew disappeared in their search for the bombers. All five bombers were also gone without a trace.

Over the years, many more ships and planes have crashed or vanished in

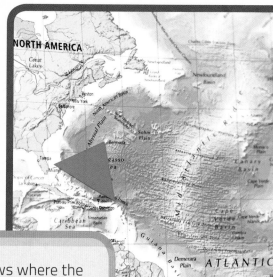

The red triangle shows where the Bermuda Triangle sits.

the Bermuda Triangle. People wonder if there is a scientific explanation. Some suggest the area has odd magnetic currents that cause strange compass readings. Another claim is that methane gas from the ocean floor causes unsteady water that ships cannot handle. A few believe the disappearances have to do with aliens living in space or underwater.

These US Navy Avengers are similar to those that went missing in 1945.

500,000
Area, in square miles (1.3 million sq. km), of the Bermuda Triangle.

- The Bermuda Triangle is an area in the Atlantic Ocean.
- It is the site of many plane and ship disappearances.
- The USS *Cyclops* disappeared in March 1918. Its wreckage was never found.
- In 1945, five US Navy bombers vanished after their compasses malfunctioned.

CHRISTOPHER COLUMBUS

Christopher Columbus was a famous explorer. During his first voyage to the New World, he reported a great flame crashing into the sea. Now historians believe this was within the Bermuda Triangle. The flame was probably a meteor. Columbus wrote of a mysterious light in the sky a few weeks later. He also wrote about strange compass readings.

13

Famed Aviator Amelia Earhart Vanishes

Amelia Earhart was one of the most famous aviators of the 1900s. But it is her disappearance in 1937 that remains a large part of her legacy. As her 40th birthday approached, Earhart decided she wanted to be the first female pilot to fly around the globe. On June 1, 1937, she and navigator Fred Noonan departed from Miami, Florida.

Their journey around the globe would have taken them 29,000 miles (47,000 km). After flying for 29 days, Earhart and Noonan landed in New Guinea. The last leg of their journey took them over the Pacific Ocean. They fought against overcast skies and rain. The pair's last communication with air traffic controllers occurred after unsuccessfully trying to land on Howland Island in the Pacific. And, like that, they vanished.

Numerous theories about Earhart's disappearance developed over the years. Some say she returned home safely and changed her name. Another theory said Earhart was a spy

Earhart was the first female pilot to fly across the Atlantic Ocean.

for President Franklin D. Roosevelt. They believed her plane crashed or she was taken prisoner on a Japanese-controlled island in the Pacific.

The most convincing theory concluded that Earhart and Noonan touched down on a remote island in the South Pacific. They survived for a time but died without being saved. Scientists have found clues on the island that possibly could be traced to Earhart and Noonan. These included tools and clothing. A skeleton found in 1940 might have belonged to one of the missing pilots. The bones were sent to Fiji. They were somehow lost or misplaced. There is hope that someday the mystery could be solved. Until then, the disappearance of Earhart remains one of the most famous mysteries of all time.

Communication was difficult during Earhart's last flight.

THINK ABOUT IT

In Amelia Earhart's day, it was a lot more difficult to track aircraft in flight. Do some research and find three examples of technology that has made navigation easier.

39
Age of Amelia Earhart when she went missing.

- Amelia Earhart was the first female pilot to fly solo across the Atlantic Ocean.
- In June 1937, she attempted to fly around the globe.
- Earhart and her navigator, Fred Noonan, disappeared in the Pacific Ocean.
- Some people believe Earhart was stranded on a remote island.

Blobs of Goop Drop From the Sky

The night of August 7, 1994, was the same as any other in the town of Oakville, Washington. That all changed at approximately 3:00 a.m. Rain began to fall from the sky. But the small town was in for a surprise. It was not rain falling from the sky, but small jelly-like blobs.

The clear blobs were small. They were no larger than half the size of a grain of rice. The blobs fell from the sky a total of six times over three weeks. After the rainfall, several Oakville residents began to show symptoms of the flu. One woman had a fever and an infection after touching the blobs with her bare hands.

The jelly-like blobs were tested. It was concluded they were a man-made material that could carry a virus or bacteria. During the testing, though, the scientist in charge discovered that the samples were missing. A supervisor told the scientist not to ask questions. So what was the mysterious goo that fell from the sky?

20
Area, in square miles (52 sq. km), affected by the jelly-like blobs.

- Jelly-like blobs began falling from the sky on August 7, 1994, in Oakville, Washington.
- Some residents reported feeling ill and having infections afterward.
- Scientists tested the blobs, but the samples soon vanished.
- Many think the blobs were part of a US military experiment.

According to one popular theory, the blobs were caused by something some people called star jelly. It is suggested that a naval bombing in the ocean 50 miles (80 km) away accidentally exploded within a school of jellyfish. The particles of jellyfish were then spread into a rain cloud.

A second theory says the blobs were part of a military experiment to test a biological weapon. Oakville residents reported seeing slow-moving military aircraft in the weeks before the strange

rainfall. The US Air Force confirmed doing practice runs in the area in 1994. But it denied any link to the blobs. There is little photographic or physical evidence of the blobs anymore. The truth will most likely remain a mystery.

THINK ABOUT IT

What do you think is the most logical explanation for the jelly-like blobs? List three possible reasons.

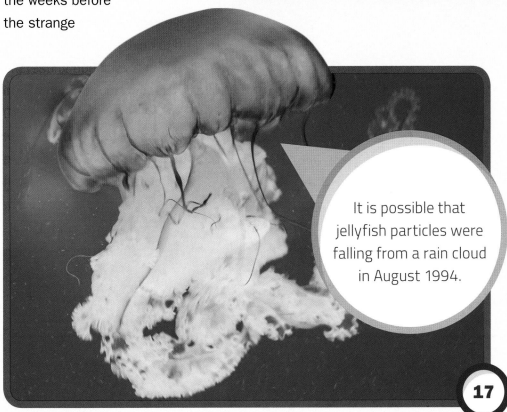

It is possible that jellyfish particles were falling from a rain cloud in August 1994.

Man Leaps From Plane and Disappears

On the afternoon before Thanksgiving 1971, a businessman in a black suit and tie boarded Northwest Orient Airlines Flight 305. The plane was traveling from Portland, Oregon, to Seattle, Washington. The man was Dan Cooper, although media outlets later called him D. B. Cooper. Once the plane was airborne, Cooper showed a briefcase to the flight attendants. He claimed it contained a bomb.

The plane landed in Seattle, but no one got off. The pilot informed air traffic control that the aircrew was dealing with a situation onboard. Cooper demanded $200,000 and several parachutes. Eventually the passengers were released. Then the plane once again took off.

As the plane flew south, Cooper put on one of the parachutes. He tied the bag of money to himself

These sketches of D. B. Cooper reflect how the passengers and crew described him.

and lowered the plane's rear stairs. Then he leaped into the night, leaving behind nothing but a world of questions.

In 1980, a boy discovered three bundles of cash while digging a fire pit in the sand just north of Portland. The serial numbers on the cash matched those on the money with which Cooper had jumped out of the plane.

Over the years, there have been thousands of leads on the mystery man. Some claim that Cooper would not have survived his jump in the bad weather. However, his body and parachute were never found.

Hundreds of men have claimed to be D. B. Cooper. While most of these claims were proven false, a few stand out. Most notably is the story of Kenneth Christiansen. Christiansen was a trained army paratrooper who worked for Northwest Orient. On his deathbed, Christiansen nearly whispered a secret to his brother, but withheld it for some reason. Was it a confession that he was Cooper? The world will never know.

36
Number of passengers aboard Northwest Orient Airlines Flight 305.

- A man named Dan Cooper hijacked a plane, demanding money and parachutes.
- Then he leaped from the plane mid-flight.
- No one has seen Cooper since or found his body.
- Hundreds of men have claimed to be Cooper, but no suspect has been identified.

19

9

Three Men Escape From Alcatraz

From 1934 until 1963, Alcatraz was one of the United States' leading maximum-security prisons. The island prison in San Francisco Bay held some of the country's most dangerous criminals. It is believed that no inmate ever escaped Alcatraz. But is that true?

On June 11, 1962, three men attempted to break out of the prison. Frank Morris and brothers John and Clarence Anglin were all serving life sentences for robbery and other crimes. In preparation, the trio created dummy heads out of a cement powder mixture made from soap and toilet paper. They even glued hair clippings from the prison barbershop onto the heads. The men also built a raft and life vests using raincoats and glue. They hid the materials each night on top of the cellblock.

Morris and the Anglins had also dug through the concrete prison walls around the vents in their cells. They used sharpened metal spoons and a makeshift drill. They played an accordion to muffle the sound. On the night of the breakout, Morris and

20

The dummy heads were painted and left in the men's beds during the escape.

29
Number of years Alcatraz held prisoners.

- Some of the most dangerous criminals were imprisoned at Alcatraz.
- Three men, Frank Morris and John and Clarence Anglin, attempted escape in 1962.
- They used dummy heads in their bunks and built a raft out of raincoats.
- The men vanished, and no one knows if they survived.

SOLVING MYSTERIES

Recently, a computer application for analyzing flood risks in the San Francisco Bay was used to study whether the inmates' escape was possible. The simulation determined the best time to launch a raft, where the currents would have taken the men, and where their debris would float ashore. The model's findings were accurate about where the FBI found the trio's paddle and personal belongings.

the Anglins escaped through the vents. They climbed the plumbing to the roof, raced across it, and slid down piping to the ground. From there, the men entered the water with their inflatable raft. The three men were never seen again.

The FBI searched the water. They found life vests, along with a sealed plastic bag containing letters and addresses. There were no signs of the men, though. The prison claimed the men drowned, but the US government has an active file on the case.

The three men escaped from Alcatraz through a vent.

10

Ship Found Sailing Without Crew Members

The winter of 1872 was known for terrible storms. The storms caused hundreds of ships to be lost or abandoned in the Atlantic Ocean. In November, a cargo ship named the *Mary Celeste* left New York Harbor. Captain Benjamin Spooner Briggs, along with his wife, daughter, and several crew members, were headed for Genoa, Italy.

The ocean waves were rough. There were strong winds and terrible storms. But the *Mary Celeste* survived. On the morning of November 25, it passed Santa Maria Island in the Azores. This is approximately 880 miles (1,420 km) from Portugal.

Mystery has surrounded the *Mary Celeste* since its disappearance.

10

Number of missing crew members and passengers from the *Mary Celeste*.

- The *Mary Celeste* left New York Harbor in November 1872.
- The ship was found off course near the Azores islands.
- Its cargo and supplies were mostly undamaged, but no one was onboard.
- Many think the crew abandoned the ship because of a gas smell and a fear that the ship would explode.

THE *FLYING DUTCHMAN*

The *Flying Dutchman* remains the most famous ghost ship story of all time. According to legend, the captain of the 1600s ship and his crew faced a storm. The captain swore he could handle whatever was thrown at him. The ship hit a rock and sank. The entire crew died. The ghostly crew members are now said to sail forever as punishment.

It was the last position recorded in the ship's log.

Ten days later, on December 4, the British ship *Dei Gratia* discovered the *Mary Celeste* in choppy waters. The ship was nearly 400 miles (640 km) off course. The captain of the *Dei Gratia* sent his crew to investigate. They found the ship abandoned.

The *Dei Gratia* crew noted the cargo of the *Mary Celeste* was intact. There was enough food and supplies to last six months. Navigational instruments and maps were missing. The *Dei Gratia* brought the *Mary Celeste* into the nearest port.

It is unclear what happened to the crew of the *Mary Celeste*. Theories range from a pirate kidnapping to a sudden earthquake or waterspout washing everyone overboard. The most likely theory involves the ship's dangerous cargo. There were barrels of industrial alcohol. Perhaps fearing the alcohol's fumes would cause an explosion, the crew abandoned ship in the lifeboat, only to be caught in a storm and lost at sea.

The Curse of the Evil Crater

In 1949, geologist Vadim Kolpakov set off into the rugged wilderness of Siberia to map the region. He did not realize that he was about to stumble across one of the most puzzling sites in modern record. As Kolpakov trekked deeper into the wilderness, the local people in the area, the Yakut, met him with warnings. They spoke of an evil place in the woods. It was a place that even deer and other animals feared.

Kolpakov did not listen to their warnings. He was a man of science. Legends did not scare him. Instead, he pressed onward. Soon, he discovered the cause of the Yakut's fears. An enormous mound rose from the trees. It was as tall as a 25-story building.

The mound's volcano-like cone was 262 feet (80 m) tall and 492 feet (150 m) wide. The sight of it shocked Kolpakov. But he was amazed by

The Yakut warned Kolpakov of a place where people became ill or disappeared without a trace.

The crater is found in the Irkutsk region of Siberia.

its perfect shape and size. Its legend and mysterious nature grew. In 2005, an expedition set out in search of answers. The leader of the expedition tragically died of a heart attack miles from the crater's site.

Many wild theories have been presented over the years. Some believe the crater was created by an ancient civilization. Others think it was a top-secret Soviet labor camp. Still others think a UFO caused it.

Only two scientific theories for the crater's existence remain. One is that a meteorite strike caused it. The other theory is that the crater is really a hidden volcano beneath Earth's surface. However, recent samples and scientific research found no meteor materials. And the nearest volcano is thousands of

miles away. The truth of the crater remains a secret. Until its questions can be answered, it will remain the most mysterious place in Russia.

250
Estimated age of crater as noted by modern scientists.

- Geologist Vadim Kolpakov discovered a crater in the Siberian wilderness.
- It was an area where local people claimed evil things happened.
- One researcher died of a heart attack miles from the crater.
- The crater is said to be a hidden volcano or the site of a meteorite strike.

Lost Treasure Hidden on Oak Island

It was 1795 in Nova Scotia. Eighteen-year-old Daniel McGinnis spied strange lights on Oak Island. Out of curiosity, he went in search of them. He found a clearing with a circular impression in the ground and a system of ropes and pulleys hanging from a nearby tree. This began the legend of the Oak Island lost treasure.

McGinnis rounded up two friends. Curious about the strange site, they began to dig. But all they found were layers of wood, stone, and dirt. The search began again in 1804. Eighty-eight feet (27 m) down, the three men found a stone slab with symbols on it. According to one linguist, the stone said there were two million British pounds buried 40 feet (12 m) down.

The area became more of a mystery as people dug deeper. There were layers of wood, putty, and charcoal. After a certain layer of oak was lifted, a booby trap was sprung. The hole filled with water. Later, crews found a cement vault. The vault had unknown contents and was more than 150 feet (46 m) deep. A scrap of paper with unknown letter combinations was also found.

LOST TREASURE

Stories of lost treasure have always fascinated people. One story involves the RMS *Republic*, a ship made by the same builders as the RMS *Titanic*. The *Republic* sank three years before the *Titanic*. While most of the passengers survived, the cargo did not. Legend says nearly $4 million in gold was on the ship. The ship was found in 1981. But the supposed treasure was not.

People, including Franklin D. Roosevelt (third from right), and companies from all around began to dig for the lost treasure.

140
Area, in acres (57 ha), of Oak Island.

- Eighteen-year-old Daniel McGinnis discovered the site in 1795.
- Treasure hunters have found layers of wood and metal, as well as booby traps.
- Many people have lost their lives searching for the treasure.
- Some think there could be pirate treasure buried beneath the island.

Discoveries continued. People found a pair of scissors believed to be made in Mexico. They found handmade nails and a pair of leather shoes. In 1976, images from a camera lowered into the hole discovered a severed hand and a human body. The camera also found three chests that possibly contained treasure. But before searchers got to them, the tunnel collapsed.

To this day, treasure hunters continue to search the Money Pit. People think anything from pirate treasure to a sunken Viking ship is hidden on the island. Though many lives were lost in the hope of finding riches, the true treasure on Oak Island remains buried beneath the ground.

Fact Sheet

- Unsolved mysteries have existed since ancient times. One such mystery, the Lost City of Atlantis, claims that a mythical city written about by Greek philosopher Plato once existed. Atlantis, considered a peaceful society, sank to the bottom of the ocean. No trace of the city has ever been found.

- In 1952, the US Air Force began a program called Project Blue Book that recorded and investigated UFO sightings. Project Blue Book became the longest-running series of inquiries into UFOs. Between 1952 and 1969, it compiled more than 12,000 sightings or events that were deemed either "identified" or "unidentified."

- Nearly 20 percent of Americans claim to have seen a ghost. One of the most haunted places in the United States is the US Civil War battlefield in Gettysburg, Pennsylvania, where more than 7,000 soldiers died. Numerous ghostly encounters with men in uniform have been reported.

- Treasure hunters continue to search for missing gold. In Florida, there is a stretch of coast known as Treasure Coast because gold goblets and silver plates wash up onto the shore from the ocean. The treasure comes from a fleet of 11 Spanish ships that sailed to the New World in 1715, but ten ships sank during hurricane season. Four of the treasure-filled ships are still missing.

- Jelly-like blobs are not the only strange items to have fallen from the sky. Rains of spiders, frogs, blood, and even golf balls have been reported. The typical explanation involves a tornado or weather phenomenon lifting the objects into the sky and depositing them miles away.

- One of the most baffling mysteries involving a ship occurred in 1947 aboard the *SS Ourang Medan*. An SOS message was sent out from the ship claiming the captain and crew were dead, and the man sending the message died during the transmission. The ship and its crew were discovered, but no conclusion or reason for their deaths were found.

Glossary

aviators
The people who operate an aircraft.

biological weapon
A harmful living thing, such as a germ, that is used as a weapon in war.

civilization
A well-developed society.

colonists
People living in a distant land with ties to another nation.

expedition
A journey for a particular purpose.

geologist
Scientist who studies the history of the earth and its life recorded in rocks.

log
The record of a ship's voyage.

navigator
An officer on a ship or aircraft responsible for directing its course.

paratrooper
A soldier who is trained and equipped to parachute from an airplane.

settlement
A place or region that is newly occupied by people.

vault
A room or compartment for storage or safekeeping.

For More Information

Books

Lusted, Marcia Amidon. *The D. B. Cooper Hijacking*. Minneapolis, MN: Abdo, 2012.

Montgomery, Heather L. *Unsolved Mysteries of Nature*. North Mankato, MN: Capstone, 2016.

Walker, Kathryn. *Mysteries of the Bermuda Triangle*. New York: Crabtree, 2009.

Visit 12StoryLibrary.com

Scan the code or use your school's login at **12StoryLibrary.com** for recent updates about this topic and a full digital version of this book. Enjoy free access to:

- Digital ebook
- Breaking news updates
- Live content feeds
- Videos, interactive maps, and graphics
- Additional web resources

Note to educators: Visit 12StoryLibrary.com/register to sign up for free premium website access. Enjoy live content plus a full digital version of every 12-Story Library book you own for every student at your school.

Index

Alcatraz, 20–21
Anglin, Clarence, 20–21
Anglin, John, 20–21
Atlantic Ocean, 4, 12, 22

Baychimo, 8–9
Bermuda Triangle, 12–13
Briggs, Benjamin
    Spooner, 22

Chesapeake Bay, 4
Christiansen, Kenneth,
    19
Columbus, Christopher,
    13
Cooper, Dan "D. B.,"
    18–19

Dei Gratia, 23

Earhart, Amelia, 14–15

Florida, 12, 14
Flying Dutchman, 23
Foo Fighters, 6

Hexham, England, 10–11
Howland Island, 14

Kolpakov, Vadim, 24

Mary Celeste, 22–23
McGinnis, Daniel, 26
Morris, Frank, 20

New Guinea, 14
Noonan, Fred, 14–15
Northwest Orient, 18–19

Oak Island, Nova Scotia,
    26–27
Oakville, Washington,
    16–17

Pacific Ocean, 14–15
Pollock family, 10–11
Portland, Oregon, 18, 19
Puerto Rico, 12

Roanoke, North Carolina,
    4–5
Roosevelt, Franklin D.,
    15

San Francisco Bay, 20,
    21
Seattle, Washington, 18
Siberia, 24

UFOs, 6, 25
USS *Cyclops*, 12

White, James, 4

About the Author

Brandon Terrell is a Minnesota-based writer. He is the author of numerous children's books, including picture books, chapter books, and graphic novels. Terrell enjoys watching movies and television, reading, playing baseball, and spending every moment with his wife and their two children.

32

READ MORE FROM 12-STORY LIBRARY

Every 12-Story Library book is available in many formats. For more information, visit 12StoryLibrary.com.